CONVERSATIONS WITH MY SOUL

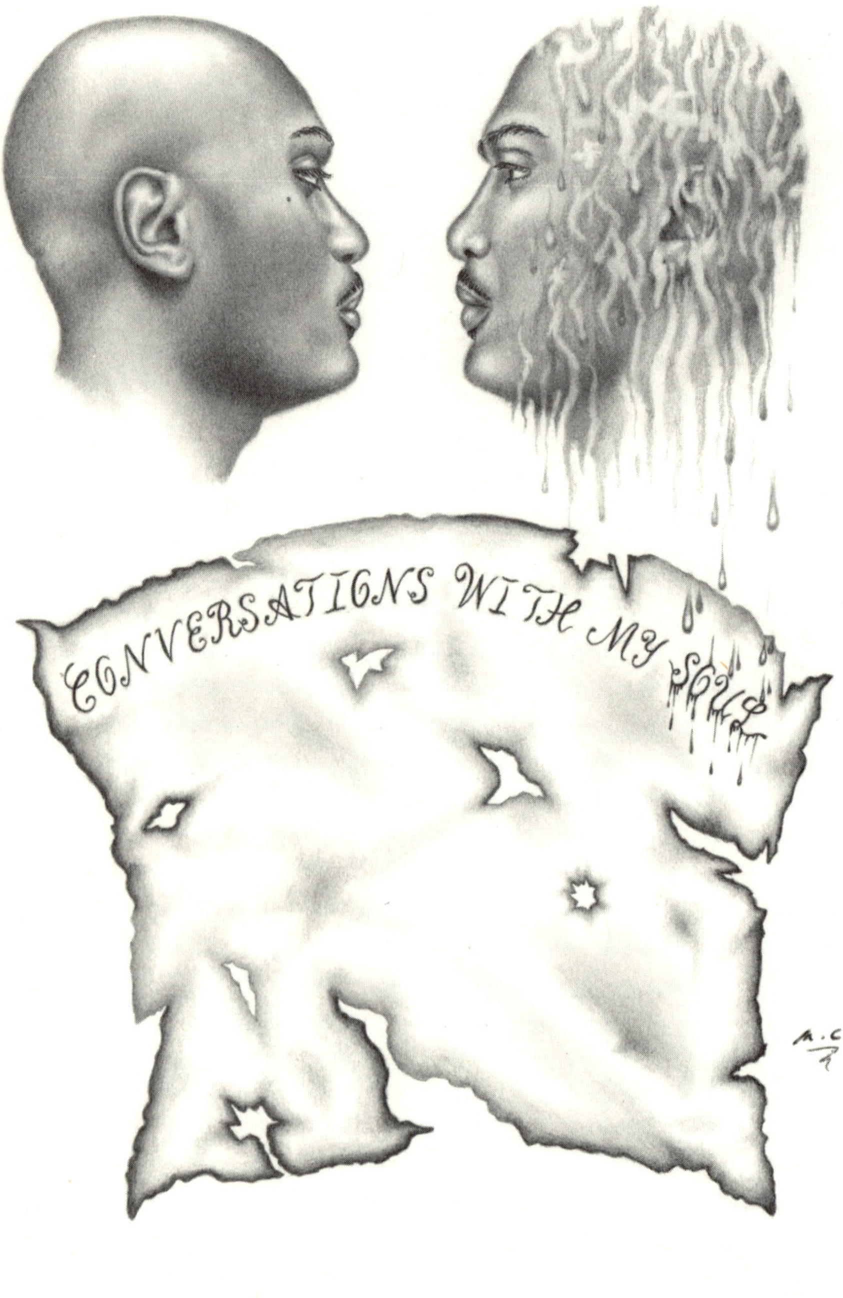
CONVERSATIONS WITH MY SOUL

CONVERSATIONS WITH MY SOUL

MESSAGES FROM A WOUNDED WARRIOR

Poems

Herman Baron III

ART BY KEVIN VEAL

I've Known Rivers PRESS

GARDEN CITY, NEW YORK

10 09 08 07 06   7 8 6 5 4 3 2 1

First Edition

Printed in the United States of America

ISBN-13: 978-0-940938-36-6

ISBN-10: 0-940938-36-7

Library of Congress Control Number: 2005936015

Book design: Cheryl Hanna

I'VE KNOWN RIVERS PRESS

Editorial Director: Geoffrey Jacques

P.O. Box 7594

Garden City, NY 11530

516-489-0120

www.knownrivers.org

inquiries@knownrivers.org

This book is dedicated

to my beautiful daughter

Amala

who never asked to but is living with

my mistakes. I'm sorry, baby girl.

Daddy loves you. And to my brother

Owen

who is following my mistakes.

Keep your head up, little bro, you'll

see the light in time.

TABLE OF CONTENTS

CONVERSATIONS WITH MY SOUL

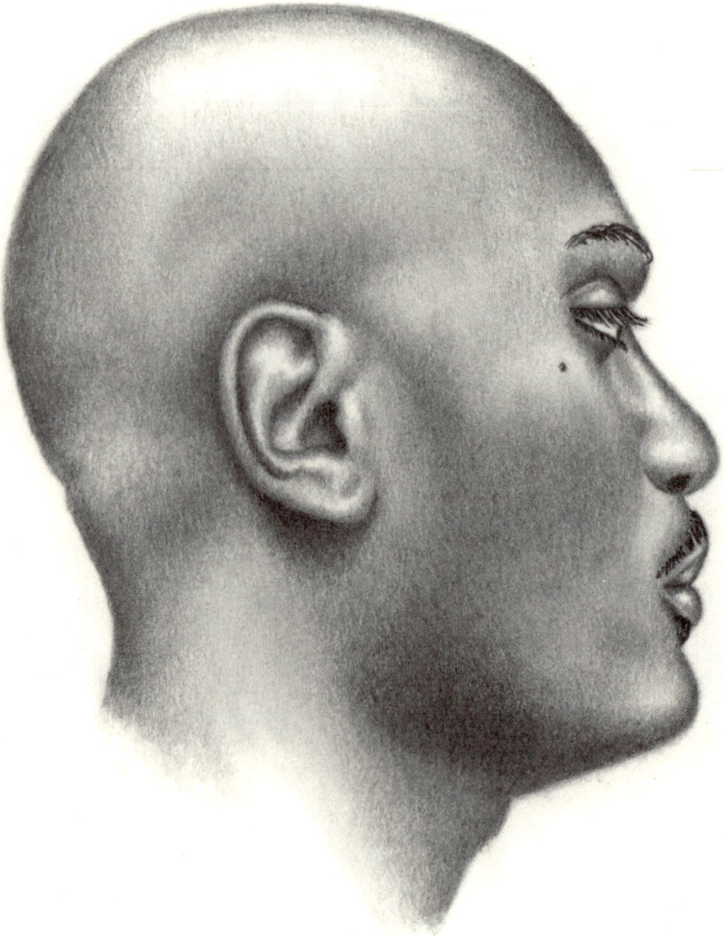

[*Introduction*]

INTRODUCTION
BY HERMAN BARON III

FOR MANY YEARS MY soul has screamed and cried to be heard, to be let out of its cage. Ironically, it took the incarceration of my physical being to release my soul. Since that time my soul has fed off my experiences of life, love, failure and pain.

The conversations that transpired between my soul and I were of great depth. They allowed me to see life in its truest form. I felt as though it was my obligation to share these conversations with the youth of today. They are the ones who are seeing a distorted vision of life, not realizing that the choices they make have consequences that will affect them for the rest of their lives. I do not expect this book to move mountains or change everybody's way of thinking, because that is not a reality. Reality is what we need for them to see in this day and age. All I can hope to achieve is that maybe through my pain and misfortune, a confused soul will gain some knowledge so that they don't make the same mistakes that I and so many others like me have made.

One final note: study the mistakes that people made in the past so that you don't incur them in your future, and retain every piece of knowledge you can because knowledge truly is power.

[*Poems*]

CHAMPION

I'm sick and tired of being sick and tired,
Having to cry in the dark,
Unable to express the emotions I truly feel in my heart,
Because it wasn't scripted in my part.
But I'm human, dammit, not an actor.
Did you think to factor into the equation
That maybe I was just good at the art of persuasion?
I spent years living behind my disguise,
Infecting my mind and body with lies,
So I could be a part of lives I knew nothing about.
I brainwashed myself into doubt
And now it's a heavyweight bout.
I'm blocking out all the screams and shouts,
I'm focused for the title fight of my life,
It's the 3rd round and victory is nowhere in sight.
Self-destruction keeps hitting me with rights
It's taking all my might just to stay in the fight.
10th round and I'm still on my feet.
My adversary is underestimating me,
Doesn't know I'm playing for keeps,
And when the final bell rings
I'll be the true champion of my life.

THINKING ABOUT THAT SPECIAL DAY IN JUNE

Thinking about that special day in June
when I produced a life,
angry at myself because I never made my daughter's
mom my wife, I allowed those
addictions to lead my life, to ruin
my life. Forced into a marriage with
the system, I just wish somebody would
stop, look and listen, and see my
tears, just look into my eyes for more
than a minute, and see that I'm scared,
not of failure, but of success. These worldly
addictions made my life a mess, I wonder
if this is God's way of giving me a test,
to let me know I'll soar beyond the rest.

BLACK MEN ARE FEARED IN AMERICA

Black men are feared in America.
NO! Black men are scared in America.
Scared to follow success, quick to
mirror impolitic indifference.
Speed balls through our veins like heroin
and cane. Systematic failure is the
message we read from our brain, quick
to understand all the bi-coastal slang
roaming through life under fictitious
names. Under our rugged shell we scream
for change, but we echo words and
music that are imbedded in our minds,
unable to find the key to unlock the door of
distortion, to clarify our vision, to
make us understand that it's society's
mission to keep us missing.

BABY GIRL

Baby girl, daddy don't know how to make
you understand. But when I was out there
running those streets, I was just being a
man. I had no plan, so it was a plan to
fail, dipping in your college fund for bail.
I want to say sorry but I don't know where
to start. And even though I'm distant now, I'm
still gonna play my part, and even though the
sun shines, my world is still dark. I wish this
system would pull this knife out of my heart. I never
felt a pain like this before. Every time I think
about you, I get numb to the core. And my
pores start to sweat and my stomach's
getting queasy, reminiscing on how you always
tried to please me: daddy look at this,
daddy look at that. No more late nights
rocking you to sleep on my lap.

LAST NIGHT I CELEBRATED THE REVIVAL OF US

Last night I celebrated the revival of us,
a friendship, a love lost.
Elated that you've given me a second chance,
honored that you saved me for the last dance,
I promise it will be the best. And when our lips
touch again you'll forget about the rest.
I just want to hold you in my arms
and relieve all your stress,
work to clean up the mess I created in your life.
This time around I'll make you my wife.
We'll honeymoon on a Caribbean beach. Not a moment will go
by with you out of my reach,
late night lovemaking under the moon,
spoon-fed strawberries and cream.
Waking up mad because this was just a dream.

HOW DO I SAY SORRY?

How do I say sorry?
How do I stop the endless nights of tears,
the fear of abandonment,
when I'm experiencing the same things myself
as I look in the mirror,
disgusted at what people
perceive me to be: Great.
But I see the truth,
the insecurities, laziness and failure.
The thoughts of an incarcerated mind can be weary
on the soul and cause my outlook on life
to be bitter and cold.
I strive to change before I get old or my soul
rests where the worms eat.
I listen when people speak,
forcing myself to contemplate and look deep within,
waiting for that spark to ignite that flame,
to warm up my soul so I can change my perception
of the reflection I see.
In this fun house called life different mirrors gave me
a distorted vision, never the truth.
So I will never let it be the final proof
of how I see myself.

THANK YOU

Did I ever tell you thank you?
Or tell you how much I love you,
For giving me the gift of expression through words–
For understanding my years of frustration–
For not turning your back on me–
For seeing the hidden talent in me?
You helped me realize what I was missing in my life,
And why I felt so incomplete.
Without you I couldn't find me.
You've helped me to grow.
You watched me progress at every stage.
You helped me place my thoughts on a blank page,
Helped me fill it with life.
I can remember the joy I felt.
You even helped me withstand the pain from poppa's belt.
You helped me to express my cry for help.
You heard my pleas,
And coaxed me into this new existence.
So every time I write
I think about you and what you have done.
I think about how I let time pass,
Without saying thank you,
Or telling you how much I love you, Poetry.

DON'T CRY NO MORE

Little girl, don't cry no more.
It's gonna be ok.
I know it feels like your life's suspended in time,
Wanting to understand your crime (being fatherless).
You are young but still determined to find your father,
While the world says "don't bother!"
Little girl, don't cry no more,
It's gonna be ok.
You don't have to sleep
With a worn out picture of your daddy
To fight away your scariest nightmares.
You don't have to sleep
With a worn out picture of your daddy,
Worn out from stained tears.
Little girl, don't cry no more. It's gonna be ok.
You don't have to be jealous of your peers,
Or conscious of staring faces in this fatherless time.
Little girl, stop your tears.
Prepare for daddy's homecoming.
Just don't start too soon.
Your daddy will be missing for a few more moons.
But please don't cry no more. Please don't. He's coming home
Soon ... soon!

MOMMA, LOST, MISS

Momma, you said the storm was over,
But I swear to God it has just begun.
I'm rapidly moving forward, but going nowhere.
I have lost the smell of the late night air.
I've lost all my hair,
Lost your personal touch,
The way you caressed my fears.
You swallowed them up like they were your own.
I loved the way just one of your kisses
Could eliminate my tears.
You taught me to stand strong,
To accept the ridicule of my peers.
I miss the way you would whisper absolutely nothing in my ear.
Damn, I miss the way you caressed my fears.
I shed acidic tears, because I'm living in my worst fear.
I shed acidic tears, because it feels like no one cares.
Damn,
I miss the way you caressed my fears, Momma.

DECEPTIVE DEPENDENCY

These sordid streets never listen when their inhabitants speak
Ignoring the signs of the dilemma they caused,
A BLACKMAN lost, and the cost was cheap.
A video and a verse is all they rehearse,
Preparations for that final ride in a hearse,
Only at that final moment do they realize that the gift
Of the fast life was really a curse.
Through their death comes a generation of clones,
Complete bodies with bones and barren souls,
The toll for their unrighteousness is a vicious cycle
Of being recycled into a demonic system,
Ostracized from a celestial world,
From relatives who no longer speak or listen.
Deceptive eyes see the symptoms
Of hunger pains and loneliness,
Offering you everything you lack or miss.
Repayment starts with a late night kiss,
Dependency is inevitable,
Becoming full of attention
Losing all sense of morals
Quarreling with themselves for what they've become,
Or when they may succumb,
For easing their pain with tainted pleasures.

MESSAGE FROM A WOUNDED WARRIOR

Sleepless nights from internal fights
Caused by my suicidal thoughts of being a parasite
Sacrificed parental expectations
I think it's long overdue for an explanation.
I was supposed to become a divine warrior,
But was wounded as I was conceived in my parents' mind.

Wounded from conception,
Birthed into deception,
So I misconstrued the battle of life,
Submerged into this concrete jungle.

Wandering aimlessly in search of my leader,
I'm pleading that these words will awaken a reader,
Fallacious information has been the key to their success,
Captured by their illusions.

Struggling to break free from this self-induced trance,
I scraped holes into the knees of my designer pants
And bloodied my fist
Just for an unconditional kiss of freedom.
A wounded warrior defending my kingdom
Fighting to make a better life for my sons and daughters
Life expectancies are growing shorter.

Increasing signs of a wounded warrior
No longer searching for my leader,
But searching for myself because self-contained knowledge
Is all that can help
Sustain the wounds.

Unmarked tombs for warriors who found out too late
Chow's at 8, rationed portions on my plate,
A message from a warrior
Wounded but not dead.

DEAR LORD

Just one of your perplexed servants dropping you a line,
Wanting to understand your definition of time
And your views on pain. I'm trying to sustain, but
I've been engulfed by the two.
Can't see the sky blue
Only the color gray,
Punishment from your hand for going astray.

My existence is living day to day,
Plagued by memories of the past.
Can't laugh at the present or talk of the future.
Were my crimes so vile that my punishment be so severe?
What happened to the comfort of your rod and staff?
And on my behalf
I want to believe
You wouldn't give me anything I can't handle,
But you lit both ends of the candle,
The flames are rising
And my inequities are highly flammable.
I felt the wrath of your anger,
But it's me, not a stranger.
So I ask you to deliver me from the danger and errors of
  my ways,
Allow me to see one more free horizon,
Instead of living my afterlife in the depths of hell.

WINDOW

I mask my anger with smiles of tranquility,
But yet it's still stained on my sleeves.
I want to believe that the world is fair,
But I look out my window
And see the world just don't care.
Now, maybe it's because my windows
And all those around me are Plexiglas
And riddled with bullets.
Or maybe it's because my window
And all those around me
See urban warfare first hand
With hand-to-hand transactions
In the midst of our day-to-day lives.

Well, I've unearthed their scheme for genocide,
And the stench of formaldehyde
Is growing stronger
By the minute.

So I shut the blinds,
Only to find myself trying to hide from the higher powers.
I saw firsthand what was done to the towers.
Don't get me wrong, I'm not afraid.
I'm just not trying to be a one-man parade,
Or the only man digging his own grave.

I'm not looking for applause,
Just a few good people to join a worthy cause.
Hello, can anybody see or hear me?
Has everyone else closed their window blinds, too?

REGRETS

I regret not loving you to my full potential.
Not realizing that my participation was essential
For the growth of us.
If I could have wrapped you in my arms
A little longer, after we made love,
Or after I told you I love you
And showered you with kisses,
I might have known what bliss is.

Instead of receiving blisters on my heart
For loving but not being loved back,
For falling into the traps of women's mysterious love acts,
I'm constantly moving from intermission to intermission.
Invisible tears glisten on my cheeks.
From the way my vacant heart speaks to my lonely soul,
I regret the fact that I'm growing old with no one to grow old with.
I regret not understanding love at an earlier age
I regret even being introduced to love.

I regret.

ABSOLUTE LOVE

Baby, I yearn to earn absolute rights to your love.
To grab you from behind and pull you close to me
So close that our bodies become one,
And our hearts beat a seductive melody
That grows louder by the minute.
In the severance of your flesh from mine
That instant loneliness is a testament of my love for you.
You've been the missing piece
in my jigsaw puzzle called a life.
I'm complete,
Made completely crazy by your every touch.
I never felt the kind of shivers
That your presence delivers
So I present you with my heart
To do with as you please.

Just be gentle.
Handle it with care.
As you know, love can be fragile.

JUNGLE FIRE

Aunt Lindamichelle
Said when hell freezes over she'll skate.
(She skated gracefully.)
A generation later the ice has melted,
I'm standing in hell,
And it's on earth,
For what it's worth.
I've been flooded with hidden agendas
While serpents pretend to be my friends,
Imposing themselves on my innocence
Which has already been stained by my own carnal sins.
I've had to survive in this ghetto jungle
Where I roamed at night to quench my animalistic cravings,
Shaving my humanity with every meal.
I made daily deals with an ever-present devil,
Disgruntled over my insipid views
That helped me to choose
The shoes I now walk in.
Talking with other creatures that have my same features,
Coming to a joint conclusion that our present lives are a
delusion.
Our only faith is to have no faith at all.
Can't waste time reading words begging for help.
I need it in a hurry.
So I smoked bible scriptures only to get a headache
from my hunger pains.
Food is scarce.
The jungle is on fire.

I'm in dire need of water,
My breath is growing shorter.
I've fallen prey to my own ways of life.
I'm in Hell and it's on Earth.

LONELY

My perpetual loneliness is my dessert
For deserting love,
For flirting with thoughts that border the passionately insane.
Waiting to attack,
Then cherishing the first kind word I hear,
I stare at other people's love through pictures,
Imagining myself in their place.
My fatuous thoughts are a disgrace.
Thinking I can take the place in another man's happiness.
So ashamed of my lewd feelings,
Dealing with my friend's awkward stares,
Leaves my soul bare.
For people to pass by and laugh,
I dress myself in remorse
Every day.
Looking to be loved,
Dreaming of hugs,
Only to wake up hugging myself,
I'm lonely with no help in sight,
So I fight my premonitions of ever being loved again,
And hold my superstitions instead.
Emotionally I'm dead,
Ignorant and lonely.

FOOD FOR THOUGHT

How can we get through today
If we don't think about tomorrow?
We are on borrowed time,
And it's of the essence
We make our presence known
And show the world from our mistakes
That we have grown.

THE YARD

The sun's light showed me
Life growing amid death.
The trees seem so close I can touch them.
But if I try I might cut my finger.
Razor sharp wire physically surrounds me.
Mentally, I build and destroy it.
Everyday the crack of a bat distracts me
From my summer daydream,
Causing me to see
Unruly teens who turned into passive adults.
They speed ahead at a steady pace,
Every lap on the track is a trip to an exotic place.
The massage in Maldives was great today.

PREMEDITATED

I smelled the scent of a woman today.
It wasn't a special fragrance,
Just the scent of an ordinary woman.
It brought back memories
Of your salty teardrops
Quenching my thirst.
You cried because you loved me,
And loved the way I made you feel.
I wanted to cry with you that night,
But my self indulgent behavior
Wouldn't let you savor that special moment.
So I watched you gag and choke on your own love.
I knew my tears could have revived you,
But I just watched you until you stopped.
I wanted to cry so bad. You know?
Just open the floodgates and let them flow.
I just didn't want to drown you with delusions.
Was I wrong for letting your love die that night?
Or should I have continued the charade
And let you drown in your own love,
Destroying your chances to ever want to love again?

No. I have to admit I premeditated
The death of your love for me.
I planned every scene
You read the script perfectly,
Even though I never gave you one.
By the time you read the final scene
I knew the crime was done,
Your love and me.

RETROSPECT

(Bed-Stuy, 1979)

A single brownstone,
Surrounded by a community of brownstones.
A single mother at home,
Throwing away her afro pick
In the process of getting a process: "A new look, dress for success."
Donna Summer singing disco hits on an 8-track.
Fried chicken, rice and spinach is Sunday's dinner,
An ordinary day for a single mother,
Raising her only son a lonely son,
Only son lonely son.
He finds comfort in Dr. Seuss
Single mother finds happiness with that tin box on her dresser,
It smells funny too,
And single mother laughs a lot when she's through.
Single mother tucks her only son lonely son in the bed,
Only son lonely son says, "I love you Mommy," and shakes his
  lonely head.
Single mother goes to bed thinking about the great man her
Only son lonely son is going to be,
Only son lonely son in bed thinking about his D·A·D,
Wondering what it would be like to be a complete
  FAM·I·LY.
Decades later, laying in prison,
The used-to-be only son lonely son has two brothers,
But they're only and lonely too,
The oldest only son lonely son produced an only daughter
  lonely daughter

Who has only a single mother to support her,
How ironic,
2005.
Now, not-single mother of oldest only son lonely son
Now sees him in his only daughter lonely daughter,
And the oldest son, only son lonely son
Is still single, living the only and lonely
Life.

BABY BRO

Baby Bro,
I want to apologize.
I need you to know
That I'm sorry
For being the one to strategize your demise
Without your knowledge or consent.
Recollecting glimpses
Of my unforgotten brother,
Seeing collages of hypocritical hugs and condescending smiles,
From the ones your momma told you to trust
When you were a child,
Confusing you on love,
Never sympathizing only criticizing
A young boy for his father's deeds,
Forcing him to proceed,
To feed his shattered ego,
By gravitating toward the wrong kind of people.
I see him running head-on into my mistakes,
Embracing them.
My wrongs becoming your wrongs,
We volleyed them back and forth like that never-ending song.
Now I'm gone, and you're trying
To come to where I'm trying to leave.
You just don't want to believe the tricks these people have up
their sleeves,
Eating away at our existence like an inoperable disease.
Blaming myself for every wrong turn you make,
It baffles the hell out of me because I don't know

How to make you do right,
To give you sight.
So I write on dirty sheets of paper,
With my blood and feelings,
Coping with not dealing with
The reality I placed you in,
My sins are teaching you not how to win,
But how to lose.
Baby Bro,
Losing you would be like losing me,
So I hope you can see my extended hands.
Embrace them,
And you'll know they are real,
Through their touch I hope you can feel
That I love you,
Baby Bro.

FACES OF DEATH

I have been staring Death in the face for so many years,
Careful never to look her directly in the eyes,
She sees what I'm doing,
So she hides herself in the things I want most:
Money, success, freedom and happiness.
She seduces me to look at her everyday.
I hate you death in the worst way.
You have forced me to stare in your eyes and see your most
horrific works,
Tsunamis, world hunger, stillbirths, black on black crime.
That deceitful bitch
Had the nerve to stare back in mine.
And she knows I've seen all the havoc and death she wreaked.
I don't even speak,
I just watch in awe at what I saw.
She sees that I'm not even scared,
But prepared to face her,
Face to face,
She knows this and toys with me.
Why can't you just let me be?
Sashaying and playing with my sanity,
Trying to steal my last breath with vanity,
My erratic breathing
Has her still scheming
And setting up ploys to destroy
A fearless witness to her heinous crimes.
She tempts me every night to take her cousin Sleep to bed
(she knows I will),

So she can ravage through my mind.
I know she's there,
But sleep just makes me feel so good,
Nothing seems real.
I feel myself slipping deeper and deeper into an eternity of sleep.
These two co-conspirators think they have completed their task,
But the taste of bile in my mouth grabs me out of my denial,
And I see that this deep sleep was not all good.
If I remember correctly everybody had on black hoods.
I've escaped her again.
I just don't know how much longer I can go on doing it:
Escape the faces of Death.

GHETTO BLUES

It's the ghetto blues,
Where we have decrepit facades,
That for so many years have been housed next to Hades.
Wiggers and Spades dying from AIDS,
The heat has taken a toll
On its dwellers lives,
As well as the buildings.
Ghetto children playing in thin soles,
Absorbing colds from a frigid winter,
Floor boards splinter and creak,
Water-stained walls speak untold stories,
Of death and oppression
Where many of its occupants took their own lives from depression,
From the ghetto blues.
It's the ghetto blues,
Everybody watches the ghetto news,
Seeing the same faces,
Different names,
Getting murdered and maimed,
Looking for someone to blame,
But only pointing the finger at each other,
Beep Beep this just in,
A thirteen-year-old mother gets strangled by her lover,
It's the ghetto blues.
The ghetto blues
Has furnished us with raggedy churches and ghetto pews,
Where a broken parish prays for atonement and redemption,
Not to mention to hit the weekly numbers,

To purchase an AC,
For the scorching summer.
Thanking God again for free lunch,
So the young kids won't die from midday hunger,
And suffer another day of the ghetto blues.
It's the ghetto blues,
Where we can't win but only lose.

TRANSCEND

I transcend
The simplest things in life.
I came.
I come.
To be one with myself
I have been broken down
Into the tiniest particles.
My most complicated articles of thought
That I catalogued in my mind
Lay next to the rest of me,
Scattered,
Waiting for a breeze to blow me
Through the universe
So I can transcend
The complexities of me.
I come,
I came,
Into this physical frame
With a name "Herman"
But no identity,
So I felt the universe offended me
By blowing my scattered particles
From place to place.
I was able to absorb and taste
The different things
Within my weightless travels.
I came,
I come.

The weight of it all
Caused me to flow together like mercury
And to create the present me,
And my identity.
I transcend.

[*Afterword & Acknowledgments*]

AFTERWORD
BY LINDAMICHELLEBARON

I HAVE BEEN PAINED by the decisions young men of African and Latin descent have been making as they define themselves as *Dawg, Nigga, Son,* names that ignore their history, their strength, their intellect, and their power. So many of this generation have embraced what previous generations of our folk once considered the negative stereotype of what it means to be Black. We, Herman's family, were conscious of these issues when we, collectively, raised Herman. We were not raising a child who would not know who he was, and from whence he's come. We gave him support and love. His father and mother, his grandmothers, aunts and uncles showed up for every event and interacted religiously. He went to church regularly. And, as he was for many years the first grandchild, he was loved unconditionally. He gave us no reason to suspect that he would embrace the streets rather than our values and belief systems.

This book represents the transformation of a young man who has been in flux. Herman's poetry affirms his decision to be more than he has known himself to be, and to become all that we have believed him to be. I believe that the reader of this book will be positively affirmed and energized. When my nephew woke up one morning, at three years old, exclaiming that "the sun is on," I named a book of my own based on his childish view of the world: *The Sun Is On.* Now my life's work incorporates many of his perceptions and realities.

He is the youth I am committed to and believe in. His poetry is powerful. Herman has proven himself to be a poet who currently seems to be poor in circumstances, but as the reader will detect, he is rich in spirit. Feel the power as you read and reflect.

DR. LINDAMICHELLEBARON, a poet in her own right, is an assistant professor of education who was a teacher and is now also a teacher of teachers. She has been the publisher, for over 25 years, of Harlin Jacque Publications. This new venture, the not-for-profit I've Known Rivers Press, has been inspired by her interactions with her nephew, Herman, during his road to redemption.

ABOUT I'VE KNOWN RIVERS PRESS

I'VE KNOWN RIVERS PRESS is the non-profit sister press of Harlin Jacque Publications. The press has been created to publish poets and storytellers who come from underserved populations–writers who lack access to literary outlets and opportunities. Our writers include poets and storytellers of color, women writers, incarcerated writers, young and elder writers. I've Known Rivers Press seeks to expose these artists to professional opportunities, writing workshops, professional mentoring and publication. The title of the imprint is a tribute to the poet, Langston Hughes, whose famous poem, "The Negro Speaks of Rivers," encompasses both the mission and the heart of our goal as publishers.

ACKNOWLEDGMENTS

FIRST OF ALL I would like to thank God for giving me the strength and courage to get through these difficult times. I'd like to thank my mother, Renee Donaldson, and my father, Herman Baron II, for giving me the gift of life and for still loving me unconditionally when I tried to destroy that gift.

Thanks to my grandmothers, Bernice Donaldson and Dorothy Baron, I love you both. Thanks are also due to my little brother Derrick and to the rest of my family. Thanks to my daughter's mother, Sophia King, for putting up with me for so many years, forgiving me so many of the feelings that I put on paper and for giving me the joy of my life, Amala.

Thanks also to Ronald Holiday, K. Everett and Ty Bosco. I can never forget my brothers in struggle who are my critics and audience: Q. Murray, M. Parks, E. Armstrong, D. Bridgeman and R. Stanley. Thanks for the encouragement and support. Extra thanks to Kevin Veal for the spectacular artwork, for helping me to bring my poetry to life and pushing me to master my art and myself. Extra thanks to Charles "Silk" Dunn for being all-around supportive and for introducing me to spoken word poetry, being a role model in these conditions and giving me and other brothers like me a guide to follow.

I would also like to thank my book designer, Cheryl Hanna and my editor, Dr. Geoffrey Jacques, for reading my work and believing in me from the start. Your support and confidence has been a blessing.

Last, but not least, I would like to thank my aunt, Dr. Lindamichellebaron, for being the shining light in my time of darkness. There are no words in the English language that can express the love and gratitude I feel for you. You are the reason I am who I am today, because without you my words would just be in a notebook somewhere. Thank you for the love and encouragement, the support and for never turning your back on me. I love you.

Yes. *"The Sun Is On."*

–Herman Baron III

COLOPHON

THIS BOOK IS SET in the transitional typefaces Rotis Serif and Rotis Semi Sans. The display face used here is Caflisch Script Bold. Mr. Veal's artwork, reproduced on the cover, the frontispiece and the pages before the introduction, is executed in graphite pencil.